50 Fall Season Recipes for Home

By: Kelly Johnson

Table of Contents

- Butternut Squash Soup
- Pumpkin Chili
- Apple Cider Pork Chops
- Sweet Potato and Black Bean Tacos
- Maple Glazed Carrots
- Cranberry Orange Muffins
- Spiced Pumpkin Bread
- Roasted Brussels Sprouts with Bacon
- Butternut Squash Risotto
- Pear and Gorgonzola Salad
- Beef and Barley Soup
- Apple Cinnamon Oatmeal
- Stuffed Acorn Squash
- Mushroom and Wild Rice Casserole
- Pumpkin Spice Latte
- Pecan Pie
- Harvest Vegetable Stew
- Baked Sweet Potatoes with Cinnamon
- Spaghetti Squash with Marinara
- Caramel Apple Cheesecake
- Roasted Cauliflower with Curry
- Sweet Potato and Kale Salad
- Turkey and Cranberry Meatballs
- Autumn Vegetable Stir-Fry
- Pumpkin Pancakes
- Butternut Squash and Sage Pasta
- Hot Apple Cider
- Spiced Pear Chutney
- Maple Pumpkin Pie
- Creamy Tomato Basil Soup
- Apple and Walnut Stuffing
- Cinnamon Roasted Nuts
- Butternut Squash and Spinach Lasagna
- Apple-Glazed Chicken
- Cranberry Walnut Salad
- Pumpkin Spice Granola

- Roasted Garlic Mashed Potatoes
- Spiced Sweet Potato Fries
- Pear and Almond Crisp
- Chicken and Mushroom Pot Pie
- Roasted Beet and Goat Cheese Salad
- Stuffed Bell Peppers with Quinoa
- Pumpkin and Spinach Frittata
- Autumn Apple and Sausage Skillet
- Caramel Apple Cinnamon Rolls
- Maple Dijon Glazed Salmon
- Sweet Potato and Chickpea Curry
- Cranberry Almond Energy Bars
- Baked Pumpkin Donuts
- Harvest Fruit Crisp

Butternut Squash Soup

Ingredients:

- 1 large butternut squash, peeled, seeded, and cubed
- 2 tablespoons olive oil
- 1 large onion, chopped
- 2 cloves garlic, minced
- 1 medium carrot, peeled and chopped
- 1 medium apple, peeled, cored, and chopped
- 4 cups vegetable or chicken broth
- 1/2 teaspoon ground cumin
- 1/2 teaspoon ground cinnamon
- Salt and black pepper to taste
- 1/2 cup coconut milk or heavy cream (optional for creaminess)
- Fresh parsley or chives for garnish (optional)

Instructions:

1. **Preheat Oven and Roast Squash:**
   - Preheat your oven to 400°F (200°C).
   - Toss the cubed butternut squash with 1 tablespoon of olive oil and spread it on a baking sheet.
   - Roast for 25-30 minutes, or until tender and caramelized, stirring once halfway through.
2. **Cook Vegetables:**
   - In a large pot, heat the remaining 1 tablespoon of olive oil over medium heat.
   - Add the chopped onion and cook until translucent, about 5 minutes.
   - Add the garlic, carrot, and apple, and cook for another 5 minutes, until softened.
3. **Combine Ingredients:**
   - Add the roasted butternut squash to the pot.
   - Pour in the vegetable or chicken broth and bring to a boil. Reduce heat and simmer for 10-15 minutes, allowing flavors to meld.
4. **Blend the Soup:**
   - Using an immersion blender, blend the soup until smooth. Alternatively, carefully transfer the soup to a blender in batches and blend until smooth.
5. **Add Seasoning:**
   - Stir in the ground cumin, ground cinnamon, salt, and black pepper. Adjust seasoning to taste.
6. **Optional Creaminess:**
   - If desired, stir in coconut milk or heavy cream for extra creaminess.
7. **Serve:**
   - Ladle the soup into bowls and garnish with fresh parsley or chives if desired. Serve hot.

Enjoy your comforting and flavorful Butternut Squash Soup!

Pumpkin Chili

Ingredients:

- 1 lb ground beef or turkey
- 1 large onion, chopped
- 3 cloves garlic, minced
- 1 bell pepper, chopped
- 1 can (15 oz) pumpkin puree
- 1 can (15 oz) diced tomatoes
- 1 can (15 oz) kidney beans, drained and rinsed
- 1 can (15 oz) black beans, drained and rinsed
- 2 tablespoons chili powder
- 1 teaspoon ground cumin
- 1/2 teaspoon smoked paprika
- 1/4 teaspoon cayenne pepper (optional for heat)
- 2 cups beef or vegetable broth
- Salt and black pepper to taste
- Olive oil for cooking

Instructions:

1. **Cook Meat and Vegetables:**
   - In a large pot or Dutch oven, heat a splash of olive oil over medium heat.
   - Add ground beef or turkey and cook until browned. Drain excess fat.
   - Add chopped onion, garlic, and bell pepper. Cook until softened, about 5 minutes.
2. **Combine Ingredients:**
   - Stir in the pumpkin puree, diced tomatoes, kidney beans, black beans, chili powder, cumin, smoked paprika, and cayenne pepper (if using).
   - Pour in the broth and stir well.
3. **Simmer:**
   - Bring to a boil, then reduce heat and let simmer for 20-30 minutes, stirring occasionally, until flavors meld and chili thickens.
4. **Season:**
   - Taste and adjust seasoning with salt and pepper as needed.
5. **Serve:**
   - Ladle into bowls and garnish with your favorite toppings like shredded cheese, sour cream, or chopped cilantro.

Enjoy your hearty and flavorful Pumpkin Chili!

Apple Cider Pork Chops

Ingredients:

- 4 bone-in pork chops
- Salt and black pepper to taste
- 2 tablespoons olive oil
- 1 small onion, chopped
- 2 cloves garlic, minced
- 1 cup apple cider
- 1 tablespoon Dijon mustard
- 1 tablespoon apple cider vinegar
- 2 tablespoons brown sugar
- 1 teaspoon fresh thyme leaves or 1/2 teaspoon dried thyme
- 1/2 cup chicken broth

Instructions:

1. **Season Pork Chops:**
   - Season the pork chops with salt and pepper on both sides.
2. **Sear Pork Chops:**
   - Heat olive oil in a large skillet over medium-high heat.
   - Add pork chops and sear for 4-5 minutes per side until browned. Remove and set aside.
3. **Cook Aromatics:**
   - In the same skillet, add onion and garlic. Cook until softened, about 3 minutes.
4. **Prepare Sauce:**
   - Stir in apple cider, Dijon mustard, apple cider vinegar, brown sugar, and thyme. Bring to a simmer and cook for 2 minutes.
5. **Simmer Pork Chops:**
   - Return pork chops to the skillet and pour in chicken broth.
   - Reduce heat to low, cover, and simmer for 15-20 minutes, or until pork chops are cooked through and tender.
6. **Serve:**
   - Remove pork chops and let rest briefly. Spoon sauce over pork chops and serve hot.

Enjoy your savory and slightly sweet Apple Cider Pork Chops!

Sweet Potato and Black Bean Tacos

Ingredients:

- 2 medium sweet potatoes, peeled and diced
- 1 tablespoon olive oil
- 1 teaspoon ground cumin
- 1 teaspoon smoked paprika
- 1/2 teaspoon chili powder
- Salt and black pepper to taste
- 1 can (15 oz) black beans, drained and rinsed
- 1 cup corn kernels (fresh, frozen, or canned)
- 1 tablespoon lime juice
- 8 small tortillas (corn or flour)
- Optional toppings: avocado, cilantro, shredded cheese, sour cream, salsa

Instructions:

1. **Preheat Oven:**
    - Preheat your oven to 400°F (200°C).
2. **Roast Sweet Potatoes:**
    - Toss the diced sweet potatoes with olive oil, cumin, smoked paprika, chili powder, salt, and pepper.
    - Spread them on a baking sheet in a single layer.
    - Roast for 20-25 minutes, or until tender and caramelized, stirring halfway through.
3. **Prepare Beans and Corn:**
    - In a medium bowl, combine the black beans, corn, and lime juice. Season with salt and pepper to taste.
4. **Warm Tortillas:**
    - Heat the tortillas in a dry skillet over medium heat or wrap in foil and warm in the oven for a few minutes.
5. **Assemble Tacos:**
    - Fill each tortilla with a portion of the roasted sweet potatoes and black bean mixture.
    - Add any optional toppings like avocado slices, fresh cilantro, shredded cheese, sour cream, or salsa.
6. **Serve:**
    - Serve the tacos warm with your favorite sides or a fresh salad.

Enjoy your flavorful and hearty Sweet Potato and Black Bean Tacos!

Maple Glazed Carrots

Ingredients:

- 1 lb baby carrots or sliced carrots
- 2 tablespoons butter
- 1/4 cup pure maple syrup
- 2 tablespoons brown sugar
- 1/2 teaspoon ground cinnamon
- Salt and black pepper to taste
- Fresh parsley for garnish (optional)

Instructions:

1. **Cook Carrots:**
   - Boil carrots in salted water until tender, about 5-7 minutes. Drain and set aside.
2. **Prepare Glaze:**
   - In a large skillet, melt the butter over medium heat.
   - Stir in the maple syrup, brown sugar, and cinnamon. Cook for 2-3 minutes, until the mixture is slightly thickened.
3. **Glaze Carrots:**
   - Add the cooked carrots to the skillet. Toss to coat in the glaze and cook for an additional 3-4 minutes, until the carrots are well-coated and heated through.
4. **Season:**
   - Season with salt and pepper to taste.
5. **Serve:**
   - Garnish with fresh parsley if desired and serve warm.

Enjoy your sweet and savory Maple Glazed Carrots!

Cranberry Orange Muffins

Ingredients:

- 1 1/2 cups all-purpose flour
- 1 cup granulated sugar
- 1 tablespoon baking powder
- 1/2 teaspoon salt
- 1/2 cup unsalted butter, melted
- 2 large eggs
- 1/2 cup milk
- 1 teaspoon vanilla extract
- Zest of 1 orange
- 1 cup fresh or frozen cranberries (if using frozen, do not thaw)

For the Topping (optional):

- 2 tablespoons granulated sugar
- 1/2 teaspoon ground cinnamon

Instructions:

1. **Preheat Oven:**
    - Preheat your oven to 375°F (190°C). Line a muffin tin with paper liners or grease the cups.
2. **Prepare Dry Ingredients:**
    - In a large bowl, whisk together the flour, sugar, baking powder, and salt.
3. **Mix Wet Ingredients:**
    - In another bowl, combine the melted butter, eggs, milk, vanilla extract, and orange zest.
4. **Combine Ingredients:**
    - Pour the wet ingredients into the dry ingredients and stir until just combined. Do not overmix.
    - Gently fold in the cranberries.
5. **Fill Muffin Tin:**
    - Divide the batter evenly among the muffin cups, filling each about 2/3 full.
6. **Add Topping (Optional):**
    - If desired, mix the sugar and cinnamon together and sprinkle over the tops of the muffins.
7. **Bake:**
    - Bake for 18-22 minutes, or until a toothpick inserted into the center comes out clean.
8. **Cool:**

- Allow muffins to cool in the pan for 5 minutes before transferring them to a wire rack to cool completely.

Enjoy your Cranberry Orange Muffins with a cup of tea or coffee!

Spiced Pumpkin Bread

Ingredients:

- 1 1/2 cups all-purpose flour
- 1 teaspoon baking powder
- 1/2 teaspoon baking soda
- 1/2 teaspoon salt
- 1 teaspoon ground cinnamon
- 1/2 teaspoon ground nutmeg
- 1/2 teaspoon ground ginger
- 1/4 teaspoon ground cloves
- 1/2 cup unsalted butter, softened
- 1 cup granulated sugar
- 2 large eggs
- 1 cup canned pumpkin puree
- 1/4 cup milk
- 1 teaspoon vanilla extract
- Optional: 1/2 cup chopped walnuts or pecans

Instructions:

1. **Preheat Oven:**
   - Preheat your oven to 350°F (175°C). Grease a 9x5-inch loaf pan or line it with parchment paper.
2. **Prepare Dry Ingredients:**
   - In a medium bowl, whisk together flour, baking powder, baking soda, salt, cinnamon, nutmeg, ginger, and cloves.
3. **Cream Butter and Sugar:**
   - In a large bowl, use an electric mixer to cream together the softened butter and sugar until light and fluffy.
4. **Add Eggs and Pumpkin:**
   - Beat in the eggs, one at a time, until well combined.
   - Mix in the pumpkin puree, milk, and vanilla extract until smooth.
5. **Combine Ingredients:**
   - Gradually add the dry ingredients to the wet ingredients, mixing just until combined. If using, fold in the chopped nuts.
6. **Pour Batter:**
   - Pour the batter into the prepared loaf pan and spread it evenly.
7. **Bake:**
   - Bake for 55-65 minutes, or until a toothpick inserted into the center comes out clean.
8. **Cool:**

- Allow the bread to cool in the pan for 10 minutes before transferring to a wire rack to cool completely.

Enjoy your Spiced Pumpkin Bread with a cup of coffee or tea!

Roasted Brussels Sprouts with Bacon

Ingredients:

- 1 lb Brussels sprouts, trimmed and halved
- 4 slices bacon, chopped
- 2 tablespoons olive oil
- Salt and black pepper to taste
- 2 tablespoons balsamic vinegar (optional)
- 1 tablespoon maple syrup (optional)

Instructions:

1. **Preheat Oven:**
   - Preheat your oven to 400°F (200°C).
2. **Prepare Bacon:**
   - Spread the chopped bacon on a baking sheet and bake for 5-7 minutes until starting to crisp. Remove and set aside, leaving the bacon fat on the sheet.
3. **Prepare Brussels Sprouts:**
   - Toss the halved Brussels sprouts in olive oil, salt, and pepper. Spread them on the same baking sheet with the bacon fat.
4. **Roast:**
   - Roast for 20-25 minutes, stirring halfway through, until Brussels sprouts are tender and caramelized.
5. **Add Bacon:**
   - In the last 5 minutes of roasting, add the partially cooked bacon back to the baking sheet.
6. **Finish (Optional):**
   - Drizzle with balsamic vinegar and maple syrup if desired. Toss to coat and roast for an additional 2-3 minutes.
7. **Serve:**
   - Serve warm and enjoy!

These Roasted Brussels Sprouts with Bacon are a perfect blend of savory and sweet!

Butternut Squash Risotto

Ingredients:

- 1 small butternut squash, peeled, seeded, and cubed
- 2 tablespoons olive oil
- 1 small onion, finely chopped
- 2 cloves garlic, minced
- 1 1/2 cups Arborio rice
- 1/2 cup white wine (optional)
- 4 cups chicken or vegetable broth, kept warm
- 1/2 cup grated Parmesan cheese
- 2 tablespoons unsalted butter
- Salt and black pepper to taste
- Fresh sage leaves or thyme for garnish (optional)

Instructions:

1. **Roast Squash:**
   - Preheat your oven to 400°F (200°C). Toss the butternut squash cubes with 1 tablespoon of olive oil, salt, and pepper. Spread on a baking sheet and roast for 25-30 minutes, until tender.
2. **Prepare Risotto Base:**
   - In a large skillet or saucepan, heat the remaining 1 tablespoon of olive oil over medium heat. Add the chopped onion and cook until translucent, about 5 minutes.
   - Stir in the garlic and cook for another minute.
3. **Cook Rice:**
   - Add the Arborio rice to the skillet and cook for 1-2 minutes, stirring, until lightly toasted.
   - Pour in the white wine (if using) and cook until mostly absorbed.
4. **Add Broth:**
   - Begin adding the warm broth, one ladleful at a time, stirring frequently. Wait until the liquid is absorbed before adding more. Continue until the rice is creamy and cooked al dente, about 18-20 minutes.
5. **Incorporate Squash:**
   - Gently fold in the roasted butternut squash, Parmesan cheese, and butter. Stir until well combined and creamy. Season with salt and pepper to taste.
6. **Serve:**
   - Garnish with fresh sage or thyme if desired and serve hot.

Enjoy your rich and flavorful Butternut Squash Risotto!

Pear and Gorgonzola Salad

Ingredients:

- 4 cups mixed salad greens (e.g., arugula, spinach, or baby greens)
- 2 ripe pears, cored and sliced
- 1/2 cup crumbled Gorgonzola cheese
- 1/4 cup toasted walnuts or pecans
- 1/4 red onion, thinly sliced (optional)
- 1/4 cup balsamic vinaigrette or your favorite salad dressing

Instructions:

1. **Prepare Salad Base:**
   - In a large bowl, toss the mixed greens to lightly coat with the dressing.
2. **Assemble Salad:**
   - Arrange the sliced pears on top of the greens.
   - Sprinkle with crumbled Gorgonzola cheese and toasted nuts.
   - Add the red onion if using.
3. **Serve:**
   - Drizzle with additional dressing if desired and serve immediately.

This Pear and Gorgonzola Salad combines sweet, tangy, and savory flavors for a deliciously balanced dish!

Beef and Barley Soup

Ingredients:

- 1 lb beef stew meat, cut into 1-inch cubes
- 2 tablespoons olive oil
- 1 large onion, chopped
- 2 cloves garlic, minced
- 3 carrots, peeled and sliced
- 2 celery stalks, sliced
- 1 cup barley (pearl or hulled)
- 4 cups beef broth
- 1 cup water
- 1 can (14.5 oz) diced tomatoes
- 1 teaspoon dried thyme
- 1 teaspoon dried rosemary
- 1 bay leaf
- Salt and black pepper to taste
- 1 cup frozen peas
- Fresh parsley, chopped (for garnish)

Instructions:

1. **Brown the Beef:**
    - In a large pot or Dutch oven, heat olive oil over medium-high heat.
    - Add beef stew meat and brown on all sides. Remove the beef and set aside.
2. **Cook Vegetables:**
    - In the same pot, add the onion and garlic. Cook until the onion is translucent, about 5 minutes.
    - Add the carrots and celery, and cook for an additional 5 minutes.
3. **Combine Ingredients:**
    - Return the browned beef to the pot.
    - Stir in the barley, beef broth, water, diced tomatoes, thyme, rosemary, bay leaf, salt, and pepper.
4. **Simmer:**
    - Bring to a boil, then reduce heat to low. Cover and simmer for 45 minutes to 1 hour, or until the beef is tender and barley is cooked.
5. **Add Peas:**
    - Stir in the frozen peas and cook for an additional 5 minutes.
6. **Garnish and Serve:**
    - Remove the bay leaf.
    - Garnish with fresh parsley if desired and serve hot.

Enjoy your warm and satisfying Beef and Barley Soup!

Apple Cinnamon Oatmeal

Ingredients:

- 1 cup old-fashioned oats
- 2 cups milk or water (or a mix of both)
- 1 apple, peeled, cored, and diced
- 1 tablespoon brown sugar or maple syrup (adjust to taste)
- 1/2 teaspoon ground cinnamon
- 1/4 teaspoon ground nutmeg (optional)
- Pinch of salt
- 1/4 cup chopped nuts (e.g., walnuts or pecans) (optional)
- 1/4 cup raisins or dried cranberries (optional)

Instructions:

1. **Cook Oats:**
   - In a medium saucepan, combine the oats, milk or water, and a pinch of salt.
   - Bring to a boil over medium heat, then reduce to a simmer.
2. **Add Apples and Spices:**
   - Stir in the diced apple, brown sugar, cinnamon, and nutmeg (if using).
   - Cook for 5-7 minutes, stirring occasionally, until the oats are tender and the apple is softened.
3. **Add Optional Ingredients:**
   - Stir in nuts and raisins or dried cranberries if desired.
4. **Serve:**
   - Spoon the oatmeal into bowls and add extra toppings if desired, like a drizzle of honey or a sprinkle of additional cinnamon.

Enjoy your warm and flavorful Apple Cinnamon Oatmeal!

Stuffed Acorn Squash

Ingredients:

- 2 acorn squashes
- 1 tablespoon olive oil
- 1/2 pound ground sausage or turkey
- 1 small onion, chopped
- 2 cloves garlic, minced
- 1 cup cooked quinoa or rice
- 1/2 cup dried cranberries or raisins
- 1/4 cup chopped pecans or walnuts
- 1/2 teaspoon ground sage
- 1/2 teaspoon ground thyme
- 1/4 teaspoon ground cinnamon
- Salt and black pepper to taste
- 1/4 cup grated Parmesan cheese or shredded cheddar cheese (optional)
- Fresh parsley for garnish (optional)

Instructions:

1. **Prepare Squash:**
    - Preheat your oven to 400°F (200°C).
    - Cut the acorn squashes in half and scoop out the seeds.
    - Brush the cut sides with olive oil and season with salt and pepper.
    - Place the squash halves cut-side down on a baking sheet and roast for 25-30 minutes, until tender.
2. **Cook Filling:**
    - While the squash is roasting, heat olive oil in a large skillet over medium heat.
    - Add the ground sausage or turkey and cook until browned. Remove and set aside.
    - In the same skillet, add the chopped onion and garlic. Cook until softened, about 5 minutes.
3. **Combine Ingredients:**
    - Add the cooked quinoa or rice, dried cranberries, chopped nuts, sage, thyme, cinnamon, salt, and pepper to the skillet. Stir well to combine.
    - Return the cooked sausage to the skillet and mix everything together.
4. **Stuff Squash:**
    - Remove the squash from the oven and carefully flip them cut-side up.
    - Spoon the filling into each squash half, packing it in tightly.
5. **Bake:**
    - Return the stuffed squash to the oven and bake for an additional 10-15 minutes, until the tops are golden and the filling is heated through.
6. **Finish and Serve:**

- If desired, sprinkle with grated Parmesan or shredded cheddar cheese and bake for another 5 minutes until the cheese is melted and bubbly.
- Garnish with fresh parsley before serving.

Enjoy your flavorful and satisfying Stuffed Acorn Squash!

Mushroom and Wild Rice Casserole

Ingredients:

- 1 cup wild rice, rinsed
- 2 1/2 cups vegetable or chicken broth
- 2 tablespoons olive oil
- 1 large onion, chopped
- 3 cloves garlic, minced
- 2 cups mushrooms, sliced (e.g., cremini, button, or a mix)
- 1 cup celery, chopped
- 1 cup carrots, chopped
- 1/2 teaspoon dried thyme
- 1/2 teaspoon dried rosemary
- 1/4 cup all-purpose flour
- 1 cup milk or cream
- 1/2 cup grated Parmesan cheese or shredded cheddar cheese
- Salt and black pepper to taste
- Fresh parsley, chopped (for garnish, optional)

Instructions:

1. **Cook Wild Rice:**
    - In a medium pot, bring the vegetable or chicken broth to a boil. Add the wild rice, reduce heat to low, cover, and simmer for 45-50 minutes, or until the rice is tender. Drain any excess liquid if necessary.
2. **Prepare Vegetable Mixture:**
    - In a large skillet, heat olive oil over medium heat. Add the chopped onion and cook until translucent, about 5 minutes.
    - Add the garlic and cook for another minute.
    - Stir in the mushrooms, celery, and carrots. Cook until the vegetables are softened and mushrooms are browned, about 8 minutes.
3. **Make Sauce:**
    - Sprinkle the flour over the vegetable mixture and stir to coat. Cook for 1-2 minutes to remove the raw flour taste.
    - Gradually whisk in the milk or cream and cook until the mixture thickens, about 3-4 minutes.
    - Stir in the dried thyme, rosemary, salt, and pepper.
4. **Combine Ingredients:**
    - In a large mixing bowl, combine the cooked wild rice with the vegetable and sauce mixture. Mix well.
5. **Assemble Casserole:**
    - Preheat your oven to 375°F (190°C).

- Transfer the mixture to a greased 9x13-inch baking dish or similar-sized casserole dish. Sprinkle the grated Parmesan or shredded cheddar cheese evenly over the top.
6. **Bake:**
    - Bake for 20-25 minutes, or until the top is golden and the casserole is bubbly.
7. **Garnish and Serve:**
    - Garnish with fresh parsley if desired and serve warm.

Enjoy your delicious Mushroom and Wild Rice Casserole!

Pumpkin Spice Latte

Ingredients:

- 1 cup milk (any kind, including dairy-free alternatives)
- 1/2 cup strong brewed coffee or 1 shot of espresso
- 1/4 cup pumpkin puree (canned or homemade)
- 2 tablespoons maple syrup or sweetened condensed milk (adjust to taste)
- 1/2 teaspoon pumpkin pie spice
- 1/4 teaspoon vanilla extract
- Whipped cream (optional, for topping)
- Extra pumpkin pie spice (optional, for garnish)

Instructions:

1. **Heat Milk Mixture:**
   - In a small saucepan, combine the milk, pumpkin puree, and pumpkin pie spice. Heat over medium heat, whisking frequently, until the mixture is hot but not boiling.
2. **Blend:**
   - Use a hand-held frother or regular blender to froth the milk mixture until it's creamy and foamy. If using a regular blender, blend the mixture in batches for a few seconds.
3. **Combine Coffee and Milk:**
   - Pour the brewed coffee or espresso into a mug.
   - Slowly pour the frothed milk mixture over the coffee.
4. **Add Sweetener:**
   - Stir in the maple syrup or sweetened condensed milk, and vanilla extract.
5. **Top and Serve:**
   - Top with whipped cream if desired and sprinkle with extra pumpkin pie spice.

Enjoy your homemade Pumpkin Spice Latte!

Pecan Pie

Ingredients:

- **For the Crust:**
    - 1 1/2 cups all-purpose flour
    - 1/4 teaspoon salt
    - 1/2 cup unsalted butter, chilled and cut into small pieces
    - 1/4 cup granulated sugar
    - 1/4 cup ice water (more if needed)
- **For the Filling:**
    - 1 cup light corn syrup
    - 1 cup packed brown sugar
    - 1/4 cup unsalted butter, melted
    - 3 large eggs
    - 1 1/2 cups pecan halves
    - 1 teaspoon vanilla extract
    - Pinch of salt

Instructions:

1. **Prepare the Crust:**
    - In a food processor, combine flour, salt, and sugar. Add the butter and pulse until the mixture resembles coarse crumbs.
    - Gradually add ice water, pulsing until the dough begins to come together.
    - Turn out the dough onto a floured surface, press it into a disk, wrap in plastic, and refrigerate for at least 30 minutes.
2. **Preheat Oven:**
    - Preheat your oven to 350°F (175°C).
3. **Roll Out and Fit Crust:**
    - Roll out the chilled dough on a floured surface to fit a 9-inch pie dish. Transfer it to the dish, trim the edges, and crimp as desired.
4. **Pre-bake Crust (Optional):**
    - For a crisper crust, pre-bake at 350°F (175°C) for 10 minutes. Remove from the oven and let cool slightly.
5. **Prepare Filling:**
    - In a large bowl, whisk together corn syrup, brown sugar, melted butter, eggs, vanilla extract, and a pinch of salt until smooth.
    - Stir in the pecan halves.
6. **Fill and Bake:**
    - Pour the filling into the prepared crust.
    - Bake at 350°F (175°C) for 50-60 minutes, or until the filling is set and the crust is golden brown. The pie may still be slightly jiggly in the center; it will firm up as it cools.

7. **Cool:**
    - Allow the pie to cool completely before slicing.

Enjoy your rich and gooey Pecan Pie!

Harvest Vegetable Stew

Ingredients:

- 2 tablespoons olive oil
- 1 large onion, chopped
- 3 cloves garlic, minced
- 3 carrots, peeled and chopped
- 2 celery stalks, chopped
- 1 medium butternut squash, peeled, seeded, and cubed
- 2 medium potatoes, peeled and diced
- 1 red bell pepper, chopped
- 1 cup green beans, trimmed and cut into bite-sized pieces
- 1 can (14.5 oz) diced tomatoes
- 4 cups vegetable broth
- 1 teaspoon dried thyme
- 1 teaspoon dried rosemary
- 1 bay leaf
- Salt and black pepper to taste
- 1 cup kale or spinach, chopped (optional)
- 1 cup frozen peas (optional)

Instructions:

1. **Sauté Vegetables:**
   - Heat olive oil in a large pot or Dutch oven over medium heat.
   - Add the onion and garlic, cooking until softened, about 5 minutes.
2. **Add Root Vegetables:**
   - Stir in the carrots, celery, butternut squash, and potatoes. Cook for 5 minutes.
3. **Add Remaining Ingredients:**
   - Add the red bell pepper, green beans, diced tomatoes, vegetable broth, thyme, rosemary, and bay leaf.
   - Bring to a boil, then reduce heat to low. Simmer, uncovered, for 25-30 minutes, or until vegetables are tender.
4. **Finish Stew:**
   - Stir in kale or spinach and frozen peas if using. Cook for an additional 5 minutes, until greens are wilted and peas are heated through.
   - Season with salt and pepper to taste. Remove bay leaf before serving.
5. **Serve:**
   - Ladle the stew into bowls and serve hot.

Enjoy your hearty and nourishing Harvest Vegetable Stew!

Baked Sweet Potatoes with Cinnamon

Ingredients:

- 4 medium sweet potatoes
- 2 tablespoons olive oil
- 1 teaspoon ground cinnamon
- 1/4 teaspoon ground nutmeg (optional)
- 2 tablespoons brown sugar or maple syrup (optional)
- Salt to taste
- Optional toppings: butter, chopped nuts, marshmallows, or a drizzle of honey

Instructions:

1. **Preheat Oven:**
   - Preheat your oven to 400°F (200°C).
2. **Prepare Sweet Potatoes:**
   - Wash and scrub the sweet potatoes thoroughly.
   - Pat them dry with a paper towel.
3. **Season:**
   - Prick each sweet potato several times with a fork.
   - Rub the sweet potatoes with olive oil, then sprinkle with ground cinnamon, nutmeg (if using), and a pinch of salt.
4. **Bake:**
   - Place the sweet potatoes on a baking sheet or in a baking dish.
   - Bake in the preheated oven for 40-50 minutes, or until tender. You can test for doneness by inserting a fork or knife into the center; it should slide in easily.
5. **Optional Topping:**
   - If using brown sugar or maple syrup, you can sprinkle it on the sweet potatoes during the last 10 minutes of baking for a caramelized touch.
6. **Serve:**
   - Remove from the oven and let cool slightly.
   - Serve as is or with your choice of toppings, such as a pat of butter, chopped nuts, marshmallows, or a drizzle of honey.

Enjoy your warm and spiced Baked Sweet Potatoes with Cinnamon!

Spaghetti Squash with Marinara

Ingredients:

- 1 large spaghetti squash
- 2 tablespoons olive oil
- Salt and black pepper to taste
- 2 cups marinara sauce (store-bought or homemade)
- 1/4 cup grated Parmesan cheese (optional)
- Fresh basil or parsley for garnish (optional)

Instructions:

1. **Preheat Oven:**
    - Preheat your oven to 400°F (200°C).
2. **Prepare Spaghetti Squash:**
    - Cut the spaghetti squash in half lengthwise. Scoop out the seeds and stringy bits with a spoon.
    - Drizzle the cut sides with olive oil and season with salt and pepper.
3. **Roast Squash:**
    - Place the squash cut-side down on a baking sheet lined with parchment paper or foil.
    - Roast in the preheated oven for 40-45 minutes, or until the flesh is tender and can be easily scraped with a fork.
4. **Prepare Marinara Sauce:**
    - While the squash is roasting, heat the marinara sauce in a saucepan over low heat.
5. **Scrape Squash:**
    - Once the squash is cooked, let it cool slightly. Using a fork, scrape the flesh to create "spaghetti" strands.
6. **Combine and Serve:**
    - Toss the spaghetti squash strands with the warmed marinara sauce.
    - Serve topped with grated Parmesan cheese and fresh basil or parsley, if desired.

Enjoy your nutritious and flavorful Spaghetti Squash with Marinara!

Caramel Apple Cheesecake

Ingredients:

For the Crust:

- 1 1/2 cups graham cracker crumbs
- 1/4 cup granulated sugar
- 1/2 cup unsalted butter, melted

For the Filling:

- 3 (8 oz) packages cream cheese, softened
- 1 cup granulated sugar
- 1 teaspoon vanilla extract
- 3 large eggs
- 1 cup sour cream
- 1 cup heavy cream

For the Apple Topping:

- 3 medium apples, peeled, cored, and sliced
- 2 tablespoons unsalted butter
- 1/4 cup granulated sugar
- 1 teaspoon ground cinnamon
- 1/4 cup water

For the Caramel Sauce:

- 1/2 cup granulated sugar
- 2 tablespoons unsalted butter
- 1/4 cup heavy cream
- Pinch of salt

Instructions:

1. **Preheat Oven:**
   - Preheat your oven to 325°F (165°C). Grease a 9-inch springform pan.
2. **Prepare Crust:**
   - In a medium bowl, combine graham cracker crumbs, sugar, and melted butter. Press the mixture into the bottom of the prepared springform pan.
   - Bake for 10 minutes, then cool while preparing the filling.
3. **Make Cheesecake Filling:**
   - In a large bowl, beat the cream cheese until smooth. Gradually add sugar and vanilla extract, beating until creamy.

- Add eggs, one at a time, beating after each addition. Mix in sour cream and heavy cream until smooth.
- Pour the filling over the cooled crust and smooth the top.

4. **Bake Cheesecake:**
   - Bake for 50-60 minutes, or until the center is set and the edges are slightly puffed. Turn off the oven, crack the door, and let the cheesecake cool in the oven for 1 hour.
   - Remove from the oven and refrigerate for at least 4 hours, or overnight.

5. **Prepare Apple Topping:**
   - In a skillet, melt butter over medium heat. Add sliced apples, sugar, and cinnamon. Cook until apples are tender, about 8 minutes.
   - Stir in water and cook until the sauce thickens slightly. Allow to cool.

6. **Make Caramel Sauce:**
   - In a small saucepan, heat sugar over medium heat, stirring constantly until melted and golden.
   - Remove from heat and carefully stir in butter, then cream. Add a pinch of salt and stir until smooth. Let cool slightly.

7. **Assemble:**
   - Spread the cooled apple topping over the chilled cheesecake.
   - Drizzle with caramel sauce before serving.

Enjoy your rich and decadent Caramel Apple Cheesecake!

Roasted Cauliflower with Curry

Ingredients:

- 1 large head of cauliflower, cut into florets
- 2 tablespoons olive oil
- 2 tablespoons curry powder
- 1/2 teaspoon ground turmeric (optional)
- 1/2 teaspoon garlic powder
- 1/2 teaspoon onion powder
- Salt and black pepper to taste
- Fresh cilantro or parsley for garnish (optional)

Instructions:

1. **Preheat Oven:**
   - Preheat your oven to 425°F (220°C).
2. **Prepare Cauliflower:**
   - In a large bowl, toss cauliflower florets with olive oil until evenly coated.
3. **Season:**
   - Sprinkle curry powder, turmeric (if using), garlic powder, onion powder, salt, and pepper over the cauliflower. Toss to coat thoroughly.
4. **Roast:**
   - Spread the seasoned cauliflower in a single layer on a baking sheet.
   - Roast in the preheated oven for 25-30 minutes, or until the cauliflower is golden brown and tender. Stir halfway through cooking for even roasting.
5. **Garnish and Serve:**
   - Garnish with fresh cilantro or parsley if desired. Serve hot.

Enjoy your aromatic and delicious Roasted Cauliflower with Curry!

Sweet Potato and Kale Salad

Ingredients:

- **For the Salad:**
    - 2 medium sweet potatoes, peeled and diced
    - 1 tablespoon olive oil
    - Salt and black pepper to taste
    - 4 cups kale, stems removed and chopped
    - 1/4 cup red onion, thinly sliced
    - 1/4 cup dried cranberries
    - 1/4 cup crumbled feta cheese (optional)
    - 1/4 cup toasted pecans or walnuts (optional)
- **For the Dressing:**
    - 3 tablespoons olive oil
    - 2 tablespoons balsamic vinegar
    - 1 tablespoon maple syrup or honey
    - 1 teaspoon Dijon mustard
    - Salt and black pepper to taste

Instructions:

1. **Roast Sweet Potatoes:**
    - Preheat your oven to 400°F (200°C).
    - Toss the diced sweet potatoes with olive oil, salt, and pepper. Spread them on a baking sheet in a single layer.
    - Roast for 25-30 minutes, or until tender and lightly caramelized, stirring halfway through. Let cool slightly.
2. **Prepare Kale:**
    - While the sweet potatoes are roasting, place the chopped kale in a large bowl. Massage the kale with a bit of olive oil and a pinch of salt for a few minutes to soften it.
3. **Make the Dressing:**
    - In a small bowl or jar, whisk together olive oil, balsamic vinegar, maple syrup or honey, Dijon mustard, salt, and pepper.
4. **Assemble Salad:**
    - Add the roasted sweet potatoes, red onion, dried cranberries, crumbled feta, and toasted nuts (if using) to the bowl with the kale.
    - Drizzle with the dressing and toss everything together until well combined.
5. **Serve:**
    - Serve immediately, or refrigerate for up to 1 hour before serving.

Enjoy your vibrant and wholesome Sweet Potato and Kale Salad!

Turkey and Cranberry Meatballs

Ingredients:

- **For the Meatballs:**
    - 1 lb (450g) ground turkey
    - 1/2 cup fresh breadcrumbs (or panko)
    - 1/4 cup finely chopped fresh parsley
    - 1/4 cup grated Parmesan cheese
    - 1 egg
    - 1/2 cup dried cranberries, chopped
    - 2 cloves garlic, minced
    - 1/2 teaspoon dried thyme
    - 1/2 teaspoon dried rosemary
    - Salt and black pepper to taste
- **For the Cranberry Sauce (Optional):**
    - 1 cup cranberry sauce (store-bought or homemade)
    - 1 tablespoon honey or maple syrup (optional, for extra sweetness)

Instructions:

1. **Preheat Oven:**
    - Preheat your oven to 375°F (190°C).
2. **Prepare Meatballs:**
    - In a large bowl, combine ground turkey, breadcrumbs, parsley, Parmesan cheese, egg, chopped cranberries, garlic, thyme, rosemary, salt, and pepper. Mix until well combined, but be careful not to overmix.
3. **Form Meatballs:**
    - Shape the mixture into 1 to 1.5-inch meatballs and place them on a baking sheet lined with parchment paper or lightly greased.
4. **Bake:**
    - Bake the meatballs in the preheated oven for 20-25 minutes, or until they are cooked through and golden brown on the outside.
5. **Prepare Cranberry Sauce (Optional):**
    - If using cranberry sauce, heat it in a saucepan over medium heat. Stir in honey or maple syrup if desired for added sweetness. Keep warm.
6. **Serve:**
    - Serve the meatballs hot with cranberry sauce on the side or drizzled over the top.

Enjoy your flavorful and festive Turkey and Cranberry Meatballs!

Autumn Vegetable Stir-Fry

Ingredients:

- **For the Stir-Fry:**
    - 2 tablespoons vegetable oil or olive oil
    - 1 medium onion, sliced
    - 2 cloves garlic, minced
    - 1 red bell pepper, sliced
    - 1 medium carrot, peeled and sliced
    - 1 cup Brussels sprouts, trimmed and halved
    - 1 cup butternut squash, peeled and cubed
    - 1 cup mushrooms, sliced
    - 1 cup snap peas or green beans
    - 1 tablespoon soy sauce or tamari
    - 1 tablespoon hoisin sauce (optional)
    - 1 tablespoon rice vinegar or apple cider vinegar
    - 1/2 teaspoon ground ginger or fresh ginger, minced
    - Salt and black pepper to taste
    - Cooked rice or noodles for serving
- **For Garnish (Optional):**
    - Sesame seeds
    - Chopped fresh cilantro or green onions

Instructions:

1. **Prepare Vegetables:**
    - Slice and chop all vegetables as indicated.
2. **Cook Vegetables:**
    - Heat the vegetable oil in a large skillet or wok over medium-high heat.
    - Add the onion and garlic, cooking until fragrant and the onion is translucent, about 2-3 minutes.
3. **Stir-Fry:**
    - Add the red bell pepper, carrot, Brussels sprouts, and butternut squash to the skillet. Stir-fry for about 5-7 minutes, or until the vegetables begin to soften.
    - Add the mushrooms and snap peas (or green beans). Continue stir-frying for another 5 minutes, or until all vegetables are tender and slightly crisp.
4. **Add Flavorings:**
    - Stir in the soy sauce, hoisin sauce (if using), rice vinegar, and ground ginger. Cook for another 1-2 minutes, making sure everything is well coated and heated through.
5. **Season:**
    - Taste and adjust seasoning with salt and pepper if needed.
6. **Serve:**

- Serve the stir-fry over cooked rice or noodles.
- Garnish with sesame seeds and chopped fresh cilantro or green onions if desired.

Enjoy your flavorful and colorful Autumn Vegetable Stir-Fry!

Pumpkin Pancakes

Ingredients:

- 1 cup all-purpose flour
- 2 tablespoons granulated sugar
- 1 tablespoon baking powder
- 1/2 teaspoon ground cinnamon
- 1/4 teaspoon ground nutmeg
- 1/4 teaspoon ground ginger
- 1/4 teaspoon salt
- 1 cup milk (any kind)
- 1/2 cup canned pumpkin puree
- 1 large egg
- 2 tablespoons melted butter or vegetable oil
- 1 teaspoon vanilla extract

Instructions:

1. **Preheat Griddle:**
   - Heat a griddle or non-stick skillet over medium heat and lightly grease with butter or oil.
2. **Mix Dry Ingredients:**
   - In a large bowl, whisk together flour, sugar, baking powder, cinnamon, nutmeg, ginger, and salt.
3. **Mix Wet Ingredients:**
   - In another bowl, combine milk, pumpkin puree, egg, melted butter (or oil), and vanilla extract.
4. **Combine:**
   - Pour the wet ingredients into the dry ingredients and stir until just combined. The batter will be slightly lumpy.
5. **Cook Pancakes:**
   - Pour 1/4 cup of batter onto the griddle for each pancake. Cook until bubbles form on the surface and the edges look set, about 2-3 minutes. Flip and cook until golden brown on the other side, about 1-2 minutes more.
6. **Serve:**
   - Serve warm with maple syrup, whipped cream, or a sprinkle of powdered sugar.

Enjoy your cozy and delicious Pumpkin Pancakes!

Butternut Squash and Sage Pasta

Ingredients:

- **For the Pasta:**
    - 12 oz (340g) pasta (e.g., penne, farfalle, or spaghetti)
    - Salt, for pasta water
- **For the Sauce:**
    - 2 tablespoons olive oil
    - 1 medium butternut squash, peeled, seeded, and cubed
    - 1 small onion, chopped
    - 2 cloves garlic, minced
    - 1/2 cup vegetable broth (or chicken broth)
    - 1/2 cup heavy cream (or coconut milk for a dairy-free option)
    - 1/4 teaspoon ground nutmeg
    - 1/4 cup grated Parmesan cheese (optional)
    - Salt and black pepper to taste
    - 10 fresh sage leaves, chopped (or 1 tablespoon dried sage)
- **For Garnish (Optional):**
    - Extra grated Parmesan cheese
    - Fresh sage leaves
    - Chopped walnuts or pine nuts

Instructions:

1. **Cook Pasta:**
    - Bring a large pot of salted water to a boil. Cook the pasta according to package instructions until al dente. Drain and set aside.
2. **Roast Butternut Squash:**
    - Preheat your oven to 400°F (200°C).
    - Toss the butternut squash cubes with a tablespoon of olive oil, salt, and pepper. Spread in a single layer on a baking sheet.
    - Roast for 25-30 minutes, or until tender and caramelized, stirring halfway through. Allow to cool slightly.
3. **Prepare Sauce:**
    - In a large skillet, heat the remaining olive oil over medium heat. Add the chopped onion and cook until translucent, about 5 minutes.
    - Add the garlic and cook for another minute until fragrant.
    - Stir in the roasted butternut squash. Use a fork or potato masher to mash some of the squash, leaving some chunks for texture.
    - Pour in the vegetable broth and heavy cream. Stir well and bring to a simmer. Cook for 5 minutes, allowing the sauce to thicken slightly.
4. **Add Sage and Season:**

- Stir in the chopped sage and ground nutmeg. Season with salt and black pepper to taste. If using, mix in the grated Parmesan cheese until melted and combined.
5. **Combine Pasta and Sauce:**
    - Add the cooked pasta to the skillet and toss to coat with the sauce. Cook for an additional 2-3 minutes until heated through.
6. **Serve:**
    - Serve hot, garnished with extra Parmesan cheese, fresh sage leaves, and chopped nuts if desired.

Enjoy your creamy and comforting Butternut Squash and Sage Pasta!

Hot Apple Cider

Ingredients:

- 1 quart (4 cups) apple cider (or apple juice)
- 1 cinnamon stick
- 4 whole cloves
- 2-3 star anise (optional)
- 1 orange, sliced
- 1 tablespoon brown sugar or honey (optional, adjust to taste)

Instructions:

1. **Heat Cider:**
    - In a large saucepan, combine apple cider, cinnamon stick, cloves, star anise (if using), and orange slices.
2. **Simmer:**
    - Heat over medium heat until it begins to steam. Reduce heat to low and let it simmer for 10-15 minutes to allow the flavors to meld.
3. **Sweeten (Optional):**
    - Stir in brown sugar or honey if desired, adjusting to taste.
4. **Serve:**
    - Strain out the spices and orange slices. Serve hot in mugs.

Enjoy your warm and aromatic Hot Apple Cider!

Spiced Pear Chutney

Ingredients:

- 4 cups peeled, cored, and chopped pears (about 4-5 medium pears)
- 1 cup finely chopped onion
- 1 cup apple cider vinegar
- 1/2 cup brown sugar
- 1/4 cup honey
- 1/2 cup dried cranberries or raisins
- 1 tablespoon grated fresh ginger (or 1 teaspoon ground ginger)
- 1 teaspoon ground cinnamon
- 1/2 teaspoon ground cloves
- 1/2 teaspoon ground allspice
- 1/4 teaspoon ground nutmeg
- 1/2 teaspoon salt
- 1/4 teaspoon black pepper

Instructions:

1. **Combine Ingredients:**
   - In a large saucepan, combine all the ingredients: pears, onion, apple cider vinegar, brown sugar, honey, cranberries or raisins, ginger, cinnamon, cloves, allspice, nutmeg, salt, and pepper.
2. **Cook:**
   - Bring the mixture to a boil over medium-high heat, stirring frequently.
3. **Simmer:**
   - Reduce the heat to low and let the chutney simmer uncovered for about 45-60 minutes, or until the pears are tender and the mixture has thickened to a jam-like consistency. Stir occasionally to prevent sticking.
4. **Cool and Store:**
   - Allow the chutney to cool slightly. Transfer to clean jars or containers and let it cool completely before sealing.
5. **Refrigerate:**
   - Store in the refrigerator for up to 2-3 weeks. The flavors will continue to develop as it sits.

Enjoy your homemade Spiced Pear Chutney as a condiment or gift!

Maple Pumpkin Pie

Ingredients:

For the Crust:

- 1 1/2 cups graham cracker crumbs
- 1/4 cup granulated sugar
- 6 tablespoons unsalted butter, melted

For the Filling:

- 1 can (15 oz) pumpkin puree
- 3/4 cup pure maple syrup
- 1/2 cup heavy cream
- 1/2 cup milk
- 3 large eggs
- 1 teaspoon ground cinnamon
- 1/2 teaspoon ground ginger
- 1/4 teaspoon ground nutmeg
- 1/4 teaspoon ground cloves
- 1/2 teaspoon vanilla extract
- 1/4 teaspoon salt

Instructions:

1. **Preheat Oven:**
    - Preheat your oven to 350°F (175°C).
2. **Prepare the Crust:**
    - In a bowl, combine graham cracker crumbs, sugar, and melted butter. Press the mixture into the bottom and up the sides of a 9-inch pie dish.
    - Bake for 8-10 minutes, then remove from the oven and let cool slightly.
3. **Prepare the Filling:**
    - In a large bowl, whisk together the pumpkin puree, maple syrup, heavy cream, milk, eggs, cinnamon, ginger, nutmeg, cloves, vanilla extract, and salt until smooth and well combined.
4. **Fill the Crust:**
    - Pour the pumpkin filling into the prepared crust.
5. **Bake:**
    - Bake in the preheated oven for 50-60 minutes, or until the filling is set and a knife inserted into the center comes out clean. The filling may still jiggle slightly but should be mostly firm.
6. **Cool:**
    - Allow the pie to cool completely before serving to let the filling set properly.

Enjoy your delicious and festive Maple Pumpkin Pie!

Creamy Tomato Basil Soup

Ingredients:

- **For the Soup:**
    - 2 tablespoons olive oil
    - 1 medium onion, chopped
    - 3 cloves garlic, minced
    - 1 (28 oz) can crushed tomatoes
    - 2 cups vegetable broth (or chicken broth)
    - 1/2 cup heavy cream
    - 1 tablespoon tomato paste
    - 1 teaspoon dried basil (or 1 tablespoon fresh basil, chopped)
    - 1/2 teaspoon dried oregano
    - 1/4 teaspoon sugar (optional, to balance acidity)
    - Salt and black pepper to taste
    - Fresh basil leaves for garnish (optional)
- **For Garnish (Optional):**
    - Grated Parmesan cheese
    - Croutons
    - A drizzle of cream

Instructions:

1. **Sauté Vegetables:**
    - Heat olive oil in a large pot over medium heat. Add chopped onion and cook until translucent, about 5 minutes.
    - Add minced garlic and cook for another minute until fragrant.
2. **Add Tomatoes and Broth:**
    - Stir in crushed tomatoes, vegetable broth, tomato paste, dried basil, and dried oregano. Bring to a simmer and cook for 15-20 minutes to allow the flavors to meld.
3. **Blend Soup:**
    - Use an immersion blender to puree the soup directly in the pot until smooth. Alternatively, carefully transfer the soup in batches to a blender and blend until smooth, then return to the pot.
4. **Add Cream and Season:**
    - Stir in heavy cream and add sugar if desired. Season with salt and black pepper to taste. Heat through until hot, but do not boil.
5. **Serve:**
    - Ladle soup into bowls. Garnish with fresh basil leaves, grated Parmesan cheese, croutons, or a drizzle of cream if desired.

Enjoy your rich and comforting Creamy Tomato Basil Soup!

Apple and Walnut Stuffing

Ingredients:

- 4 cups bread cubes (preferably day-old or toasted)
- 2 tablespoons butter
- 1 medium onion, chopped
- 2 celery stalks, chopped
- 2 medium apples, peeled, cored, and diced
- 1/2 cup walnuts, chopped
- 1/2 cup dried cranberries (optional)
- 1 cup chicken or vegetable broth
- 1 teaspoon dried sage
- 1/2 teaspoon dried thyme
- 1/4 teaspoon ground black pepper
- Salt to taste
- 2 tablespoons fresh parsley, chopped (optional)

Instructions:

1. **Preheat Oven:**
   - Preheat your oven to 350°F (175°C).
2. **Prepare Bread Cubes:**
   - If not using pre-toasted bread, spread bread cubes on a baking sheet and toast in the oven for 10 minutes, or until lightly browned. Set aside.
3. **Sauté Vegetables:**
   - In a large skillet, melt butter over medium heat. Add chopped onion and celery and cook until tender, about 5 minutes.
   - Stir in the diced apples and cook for another 3-4 minutes, until apples begin to soften.
4. **Combine Ingredients:**
   - In a large bowl, combine the toasted bread cubes, sautéed vegetables and apples, walnuts, and dried cranberries (if using). Mix well.
5. **Add Broth and Seasonings:**
   - Stir in the chicken or vegetable broth, dried sage, dried thyme, black pepper, and salt. Mix until the bread is evenly moistened.
6. **Bake Stuffing:**
   - Transfer the stuffing to a greased baking dish. Cover with foil and bake in the preheated oven for 30 minutes.
   - Remove the foil and bake for an additional 10-15 minutes, or until the top is golden and crispy.
7. **Garnish and Serve:**
   - Garnish with chopped fresh parsley if desired. Serve hot.

Enjoy your flavorful and hearty Apple and Walnut Stuffing!

Cinnamon Roasted Nuts

Ingredients:

- 2 cups mixed nuts (such as almonds, cashews, pecans, and walnuts)
- 2 tablespoons olive oil or melted coconut oil
- 1/4 cup granulated sugar (or coconut sugar)
- 1 teaspoon ground cinnamon
- 1/4 teaspoon ground nutmeg (optional)
- 1/4 teaspoon salt
- 1 tablespoon honey or maple syrup (optional, for extra sweetness)

Instructions:

1. **Preheat Oven:**
   - Preheat your oven to 350°F (175°C). Line a baking sheet with parchment paper or a silicone mat.
2. **Prepare Nuts:**
   - In a large bowl, toss the mixed nuts with olive oil or melted coconut oil until evenly coated.
3. **Add Spices and Sweetener:**
   - In a small bowl, mix granulated sugar, ground cinnamon, nutmeg (if using), and salt. Sprinkle this mixture over the nuts and toss to coat evenly.
   - If using honey or maple syrup, drizzle it over the nuts and toss again.
4. **Roast Nuts:**
   - Spread the nuts in a single layer on the prepared baking sheet.
   - Roast in the preheated oven for 10-15 minutes, stirring once or twice, until the nuts are golden and fragrant. Watch carefully to avoid burning.
5. **Cool and Store:**
   - Allow the nuts to cool completely on the baking sheet. They will become crispier as they cool.
   - Store in an airtight container for up to 2 weeks.

Enjoy your crunchy and aromatic Cinnamon Roasted Nuts!

Butternut Squash and Spinach Lasagna

Ingredients:

For the Butternut Squash Mixture:

- 1 medium butternut squash, peeled, seeded, and cubed (about 4 cups)
- 2 tablespoons olive oil
- Salt and black pepper to taste
- 1/2 teaspoon ground nutmeg

For the Spinach Mixture:

- 1 tablespoon olive oil
- 1 medium onion, chopped
- 2 cloves garlic, minced
- 5 cups fresh spinach, chopped (or 1 package frozen spinach, thawed and drained)
- Salt and black pepper to taste

For the Ricotta Mixture:

- 15 oz (425g) ricotta cheese
- 1 cup grated Parmesan cheese
- 1 large egg
- 1/4 cup chopped fresh basil or parsley (optional)

For the Lasagna Assembly:

- 9-12 lasagna noodles (preferably no-boil or pre-cooked)
- 2 cups shredded mozzarella cheese
- 1-2 cups marinara sauce (store-bought or homemade)
- Extra grated Parmesan cheese for topping

Instructions:

1. **Prepare Butternut Squash:**
   - Preheat your oven to 400°F (200°C).
   - Toss the butternut squash cubes with olive oil, salt, black pepper, and nutmeg. Spread in a single layer on a baking sheet.
   - Roast for 25-30 minutes, or until tender and lightly caramelized. Allow to cool slightly, then mash or blend until smooth.
2. **Prepare Spinach Mixture:**
   - While the squash is roasting, heat olive oil in a large skillet over medium heat. Add the onion and cook until translucent, about 5 minutes.
   - Add the garlic and cook for another minute.

- Stir in the spinach and cook until wilted and any excess moisture is evaporated. Season with salt and black pepper. Set aside.
3. **Prepare Ricotta Mixture:**
    - In a bowl, combine ricotta cheese, grated Parmesan, egg, and chopped basil or parsley (if using). Mix well.
4. **Assemble Lasagna:**
    - Spread a thin layer of marinara sauce on the bottom of a 9x13-inch baking dish.
    - Place a layer of lasagna noodles over the sauce.
    - Spread half of the ricotta mixture over the noodles, followed by half of the roasted butternut squash mixture, and then half of the spinach mixture.
    - Sprinkle with 1/3 of the shredded mozzarella cheese.
    - Repeat the layers: noodles, remaining ricotta mixture, remaining butternut squash, remaining spinach, and another 1/3 of the mozzarella cheese.
    - Top with a final layer of noodles, marinara sauce, and the remaining mozzarella cheese. Sprinkle extra Parmesan cheese over the top.
5. **Bake:**
    - Cover with aluminum foil and bake in the preheated oven for 25 minutes.
    - Remove the foil and bake for an additional 15-20 minutes, or until the top is golden and bubbly.
    - Let the lasagna rest for 10 minutes before serving.

Enjoy your creamy and satisfying Butternut Squash and Spinach Lasagna!

Apple-Glazed Chicken

Ingredients:

- 4 boneless, skinless chicken breasts
- 1 tablespoon olive oil
- Salt and black pepper to taste

For the Apple Glaze:

- 1 cup apple cider or apple juice
- 1/4 cup apple cider vinegar
- 1/4 cup brown sugar
- 1 tablespoon Dijon mustard
- 1 teaspoon ground cinnamon
- 1/2 teaspoon ground ginger
- 1/2 teaspoon cornstarch (optional, for thickening)

Instructions:

1. **Prepare Chicken:**
    - Season chicken breasts with salt and black pepper.
2. **Cook Chicken:**
    - Heat olive oil in a large skillet over medium-high heat.
    - Add the chicken breasts and cook for 6-7 minutes on each side, or until the internal temperature reaches 165°F (75°C) and the chicken is cooked through. Remove from the skillet and set aside.
3. **Make Apple Glaze:**
    - In the same skillet, add apple cider, apple cider vinegar, brown sugar, Dijon mustard, cinnamon, and ginger. Bring to a simmer over medium heat.
    - Cook, stirring occasionally, for about 5-10 minutes, until the glaze reduces and thickens slightly. If you prefer a thicker glaze, dissolve cornstarch in a tablespoon of water and stir it into the glaze. Cook for an additional 2-3 minutes until thickened.
4. **Glaze Chicken:**
    - Return the cooked chicken breasts to the skillet, turning to coat with the apple glaze. Cook for an additional 2-3 minutes, allowing the glaze to adhere to the chicken.
5. **Serve:**
    - Serve the chicken hot, drizzled with extra apple glaze from the skillet.

Enjoy your sweet and savory Apple-Glazed Chicken!

Cranberry Walnut Salad

Ingredients:

For the Salad:

- 6 cups mixed salad greens (such as spinach, arugula, and romaine)
- 1 cup fresh or dried cranberries
- 1/2 cup walnuts, toasted and roughly chopped
- 1/2 cup crumbled feta cheese (or goat cheese)
- 1/4 red onion, thinly sliced
- 1 apple, cored and thinly sliced (optional)

For the Dressing:

- 1/4 cup extra virgin olive oil
- 2 tablespoons balsamic vinegar
- 1 tablespoon honey or maple syrup
- 1 teaspoon Dijon mustard
- Salt and black pepper to taste

Instructions:

1. **Prepare the Salad:**
   - In a large salad bowl, combine the mixed salad greens, cranberries, toasted walnuts, crumbled feta cheese, and red onion. Add apple slices if using.
2. **Make the Dressing:**
   - In a small bowl or jar, whisk together the olive oil, balsamic vinegar, honey or maple syrup, Dijon mustard, salt, and black pepper until well combined.
3. **Toss the Salad:**
   - Drizzle the dressing over the salad and toss gently to coat everything evenly.
4. **Serve:**
   - Serve immediately, or refrigerate the salad and dressing separately until ready to serve. Toss again before serving if refrigerated.

Enjoy your crisp and flavorful Cranberry Walnut Salad!

Pumpkin Spice Granola

Ingredients:

- 3 cups old-fashioned rolled oats
- 1 cup nuts (such as almonds, pecans, or walnuts), chopped
- 1/2 cup pumpkin seeds (pepitas)
- 1/2 cup honey or maple syrup
- 1/4 cup coconut oil or melted butter
- 1/2 cup canned pumpkin puree
- 1/4 cup brown sugar
- 1 teaspoon ground cinnamon
- 1/2 teaspoon ground nutmeg
- 1/4 teaspoon ground ginger
- 1/4 teaspoon ground cloves
- 1/2 teaspoon vanilla extract
- 1/2 cup dried cranberries or raisins (optional)

Instructions:

1. **Preheat Oven:**
   - Preheat your oven to 350°F (175°C). Line a baking sheet with parchment paper.
2. **Mix Dry Ingredients:**
   - In a large bowl, combine rolled oats, chopped nuts, and pumpkin seeds.
3. **Prepare Wet Ingredients:**
   - In a separate bowl, whisk together honey (or maple syrup), coconut oil (or melted butter), pumpkin puree, brown sugar, cinnamon, nutmeg, ginger, cloves, and vanilla extract until smooth.
4. **Combine and Coat:**
   - Pour the wet mixture over the dry ingredients and stir until everything is evenly coated.
5. **Bake:**
   - Spread the mixture evenly on the prepared baking sheet. Bake for 20-25 minutes, stirring halfway through, until golden brown and crunchy.
6. **Cool and Add Extras:**
   - Let the granola cool completely on the baking sheet. It will become crispier as it cools.
   - Once cooled, stir in dried cranberries or raisins if desired.
7. **Store:**
   - Store in an airtight container for up to 2 weeks.

Enjoy your homemade Pumpkin Spice Granola as a breakfast or snack!

Roasted Garlic Mashed Potatoes

Ingredients:

- 2 lbs (900g) potatoes (e.g., Yukon Gold or Russet), peeled and cubed
- 1 whole head garlic
- 2 tablespoons olive oil
- 1/2 cup heavy cream
- 4 tablespoons unsalted butter
- Salt and black pepper to taste
- Chopped fresh parsley for garnish (optional)

Instructions:

1. **Roast Garlic:**
   - Preheat your oven to 400°F (200°C).
   - Slice the top off the garlic head, drizzle with olive oil, and wrap in aluminum foil.
   - Roast in the oven for 35-40 minutes, until the garlic is soft and caramelized. Let cool slightly, then squeeze out the roasted garlic cloves from their skins.
2. **Cook Potatoes:**
   - Place the peeled and cubed potatoes in a large pot and cover with cold water. Add a pinch of salt.
   - Bring to a boil and cook until the potatoes are tender, about 15-20 minutes. Drain well.
3. **Mash Potatoes:**
   - Return the drained potatoes to the pot. Add the roasted garlic, heavy cream, and butter.
   - Mash until smooth and creamy, using a potato masher or ricer. Adjust the texture by adding more cream if needed.
4. **Season:**
   - Season with salt and black pepper to taste. Mix well.
5. **Serve:**
   - Garnish with chopped fresh parsley if desired. Serve hot.

Enjoy your creamy and flavorful Roasted Garlic Mashed Potatoes!

Spiced Sweet Potato Fries

Ingredients:

- 2 large sweet potatoes, peeled and cut into fries
- 2 tablespoons olive oil
- 1 teaspoon smoked paprika
- 1/2 teaspoon ground cumin
- 1/2 teaspoon garlic powder
- 1/2 teaspoon onion powder
- 1/4 teaspoon ground cinnamon
- 1/4 teaspoon ground black pepper
- 1/4 teaspoon salt
- 1/4 teaspoon cayenne pepper (optional, for extra heat)

Instructions:

1. **Preheat Oven:**
   - Preheat your oven to 425°F (220°C). Line a baking sheet with parchment paper or a silicone mat.
2. **Prepare Fries:**
   - In a large bowl, toss the sweet potato fries with olive oil until evenly coated.
3. **Season:**
   - In a small bowl, mix together smoked paprika, ground cumin, garlic powder, onion powder, cinnamon, black pepper, salt, and cayenne pepper (if using).
   - Sprinkle the spice mixture over the sweet potato fries and toss to coat evenly.
4. **Bake:**
   - Spread the seasoned fries in a single layer on the prepared baking sheet. Avoid overcrowding for crispier results.
   - Bake for 25-30 minutes, flipping halfway through, until the fries are golden and crispy.
5. **Serve:**
   - Serve hot with your favorite dipping sauce.

Enjoy your flavorful and crispy Spiced Sweet Potato Fries!

Pear and Almond Crisp

Ingredients:

For the Filling:

- 4 ripe pears, peeled, cored, and sliced
- 1/4 cup granulated sugar
- 1 tablespoon all-purpose flour
- 1/2 teaspoon ground cinnamon
- 1/4 teaspoon ground nutmeg
- 1 tablespoon lemon juice

For the Crisp Topping:

- 1/2 cup rolled oats
- 1/2 cup all-purpose flour
- 1/3 cup sliced almonds
- 1/3 cup brown sugar
- 1/4 cup unsalted butter, cold and cut into small pieces
- 1/4 teaspoon salt

Instructions:

1. **Preheat Oven:**
   - Preheat your oven to 350°F (175°C). Grease a 9-inch baking dish.
2. **Prepare the Filling:**
   - In a large bowl, toss the sliced pears with granulated sugar, flour, cinnamon, nutmeg, and lemon juice until evenly coated.
   - Transfer the pear mixture to the prepared baking dish.
3. **Prepare the Crisp Topping:**
   - In a separate bowl, combine rolled oats, flour, sliced almonds, brown sugar, and salt.
   - Add the cold butter pieces and use a pastry cutter or your fingers to mix until the mixture resembles coarse crumbs.
4. **Assemble and Bake:**
   - Sprinkle the crisp topping evenly over the pear filling.
   - Bake in the preheated oven for 35-40 minutes, or until the topping is golden brown and the filling is bubbling.
5. **Cool and Serve:**
   - Let the crisp cool slightly before serving. It's great on its own or with a scoop of vanilla ice cream.

Enjoy your warm and comforting Pear and Almond Crisp!

Chicken and Mushroom Pot Pie

Ingredients:

For the Filling:

- 1 lb (450g) boneless, skinless chicken breasts or thighs, diced
- 2 tablespoons olive oil
- 1 medium onion, chopped
- 2 cloves garlic, minced
- 1 cup mushrooms, sliced
- 1 cup carrots, diced
- 1 cup frozen peas
- 1/4 cup all-purpose flour
- 1 cup chicken broth
- 1/2 cup milk or heavy cream
- 1 teaspoon dried thyme
- 1 teaspoon dried rosemary
- Salt and black pepper to taste

For the Pie Crust:

- 1 package (14.1 oz) refrigerated pie crusts (or homemade, if preferred)
- 1 egg, beaten (for egg wash)

Instructions:

1. **Preheat Oven:**
    - Preheat your oven to 375°F (190°C).
2. **Prepare the Filling:**
    - Heat olive oil in a large skillet over medium heat. Add diced chicken and cook until no longer pink, about 5-7 minutes. Remove chicken from the skillet and set aside.
    - In the same skillet, add chopped onion and cook until translucent, about 3-4 minutes.
    - Add minced garlic and cook for another minute.
    - Add sliced mushrooms and diced carrots to the skillet and cook until mushrooms are tender and carrots start to soften, about 5 minutes.
    - Stir in the flour and cook for 1-2 minutes, until the mixture is slightly golden.
    - Gradually add chicken broth and milk or cream, stirring constantly until the mixture thickens and becomes smooth.
    - Return the cooked chicken to the skillet and add dried thyme, dried rosemary, salt, and black pepper. Stir to combine and cook for another 2-3 minutes. Stir in frozen peas.
3. **Assemble the Pot Pie:**

- Roll out one pie crust and fit it into a 9-inch pie dish.
   - Pour the chicken and mushroom filling into the crust.
   - Roll out the second pie crust and place it over the filling. Trim and crimp the edges to seal. Cut a few slits in the top crust to allow steam to escape.
   - Brush the top crust with a beaten egg for a golden finish.
4. **Bake:**
   - Bake in the preheated oven for 35-40 minutes, or until the crust is golden brown and the filling is bubbly.
   - If the edges of the crust start to brown too quickly, cover them with foil.
5. **Cool and Serve:**
   - Allow the pot pie to cool for about 10 minutes before serving to let the filling set.

Enjoy your hearty and delicious Chicken and Mushroom Pot Pie!

Roasted Beet and Goat Cheese Salad

Ingredients:

For the Salad:

- 4 medium beets, scrubbed and trimmed
- 2 tablespoons olive oil
- Salt and black pepper to taste
- 4 cups mixed greens (e.g., arugula, spinach, or baby kale)
- 1/2 cup crumbled goat cheese
- 1/4 cup walnuts, toasted and roughly chopped
- 1/4 red onion, thinly sliced
- 1/4 cup balsamic vinaigrette (store-bought or homemade)

For the Balsamic Vinaigrette (if homemade):

- 1/4 cup balsamic vinegar
- 2 tablespoons olive oil
- 1 teaspoon Dijon mustard
- 1 teaspoon honey or maple syrup
- Salt and black pepper to taste

Instructions:

1. **Roast the Beets:**
    - Preheat your oven to 400°F (200°C). Line a baking sheet with foil.
    - Rub beets with olive oil and season with salt and black pepper. Wrap each beet in foil and place on the baking sheet.
    - Roast for 45-60 minutes, or until tender when pierced with a fork. Let cool slightly, then peel and cut into wedges.
2. **Prepare the Vinaigrette:**
    - In a small bowl, whisk together balsamic vinegar, olive oil, Dijon mustard, honey or maple syrup, salt, and black pepper. Adjust seasoning to taste.
3. **Assemble the Salad:**
    - In a large bowl, toss mixed greens with a little balsamic vinaigrette.
    - Arrange the roasted beet wedges on top of the greens.
    - Sprinkle with crumbled goat cheese, toasted walnuts, and sliced red onion.
    - Drizzle with additional balsamic vinaigrette or serve on the side.
4. **Serve:**
    - Serve immediately for the freshest taste.

Enjoy your flavorful and colorful Roasted Beet and Goat Cheese Salad!

Stuffed Bell Peppers with Quinoa

Ingredients:

For the Stuffed Peppers:

- 4 large bell peppers (any color)
- 1 cup quinoa, rinsed
- 2 cups vegetable broth (or water)
- 1 tablespoon olive oil
- 1 medium onion, chopped
- 2 cloves garlic, minced
- 1 cup cherry tomatoes, halved (or 1 can (15 oz) diced tomatoes, drained)
- 1 cup black beans (canned, drained and rinsed, or cooked)
- 1/2 cup corn kernels (fresh, frozen, or canned)
- 1 teaspoon ground cumin
- 1 teaspoon dried oregano
- 1/2 teaspoon smoked paprika
- Salt and black pepper to taste
- 1/2 cup shredded cheese (cheddar, mozzarella, or your choice, optional)

For Garnish (Optional):

- Fresh cilantro or parsley, chopped
- Lime wedges

Instructions:

1. **Preheat Oven:**
    - Preheat your oven to 375°F (190°C).
2. **Cook the Quinoa:**
    - In a medium saucepan, bring vegetable broth or water to a boil. Add quinoa, reduce heat to low, cover, and simmer for 15 minutes, or until the quinoa is cooked and the liquid is absorbed. Fluff with a fork and set aside.
3. **Prepare the Peppers:**
    - Cut the tops off the bell peppers and remove seeds and membranes. If needed, slice a small bit off the bottom to make them stand upright, but be careful not to cut through.
4. **Cook the Filling:**
    - Heat olive oil in a large skillet over medium heat. Add chopped onion and cook until softened, about 5 minutes.
    - Add minced garlic and cook for another minute.
    - Stir in cherry tomatoes (or canned tomatoes), black beans, corn, cumin, oregano, smoked paprika, salt, and black pepper. Cook for 5 minutes, until heated through.

- Add cooked quinoa to the mixture and stir to combine. Adjust seasoning if needed.
5. **Stuff the Peppers:**
    - Spoon the quinoa mixture into each bell pepper, packing it in gently.
    - Place stuffed peppers upright in a baking dish. If using, sprinkle shredded cheese on top of each pepper.
6. **Bake:**
    - Cover the baking dish with aluminum foil and bake in the preheated oven for 30 minutes.
    - Remove the foil and bake for an additional 10 minutes, or until the peppers are tender and the cheese is melted and bubbly (if using).
7. **Serve:**
    - Garnish with chopped fresh cilantro or parsley and serve with lime wedges if desired.

Enjoy your flavorful and nutritious Stuffed Bell Peppers with Quinoa!

Pumpkin and Spinach Frittata

Ingredients:

- 1 cup cooked pumpkin, cubed (or canned pumpkin, drained)
- 1 cup fresh spinach, chopped
- 6 large eggs
- 1/4 cup milk or cream
- 1/2 cup shredded cheese (e.g., cheddar, feta, or goat cheese)
- 1 small onion, finely chopped
- 2 cloves garlic, minced
- 1 tablespoon olive oil
- 1/2 teaspoon dried thyme
- Salt and black pepper to taste

Instructions:

1. **Preheat Oven:**
   - Preheat your oven to 375°F (190°C).
2. **Prepare Vegetables:**
   - In an ovenproof skillet, heat olive oil over medium heat. Add chopped onion and cook until softened, about 5 minutes.
   - Add minced garlic and cook for another minute.
   - Stir in the cooked pumpkin and chopped spinach. Cook for 2-3 minutes until the spinach is wilted. Season with salt, black pepper, and dried thyme.
3. **Prepare Egg Mixture:**
   - In a bowl, whisk together eggs, milk or cream, and shredded cheese. Season with salt and black pepper.
4. **Combine and Cook:**
   - Pour the egg mixture over the vegetables in the skillet. Stir gently to distribute the ingredients evenly.
   - Cook over medium heat for 3-4 minutes, or until the edges start to set.
5. **Bake:**
   - Transfer the skillet to the preheated oven and bake for 15-20 minutes, or until the frittata is set and lightly browned on top.
6. **Cool and Serve:**
   - Allow the frittata to cool slightly before slicing. Serve warm or at room temperature.

Enjoy your flavorful Pumpkin and Spinach Frittata!

Autumn Apple and Sausage Skillet

Ingredients:

- 1 lb (450g) Italian sausage (bulk, not in casings)
- 2 tablespoons olive oil
- 1 medium onion, chopped
- 2 cloves garlic, minced
- 2 apples, cored and sliced (such as Honeycrisp or Granny Smith)
- 2 cups Brussels sprouts, trimmed and halved (or green beans, if preferred)
- 1/2 cup chicken broth
- 1 tablespoon Dijon mustard
- 1 teaspoon dried thyme
- 1/2 teaspoon ground cinnamon
- Salt and black pepper to taste
- Chopped fresh parsley for garnish (optional)

Instructions:

1. **Cook the Sausage:**
     - Heat olive oil in a large skillet over medium heat. Add the sausage, breaking it up with a spoon. Cook until browned and cooked through, about 5-7 minutes. Remove from the skillet and set aside.
2. **Sauté Vegetables:**
     - In the same skillet, add chopped onion and cook until softened, about 3-4 minutes.
     - Add minced garlic and cook for another minute.
3. **Add Apples and Brussels Sprouts:**
     - Stir in apple slices and Brussels sprouts. Cook for 5 minutes, until the sprouts start to brown and the apples begin to soften.
4. **Combine Ingredients:**
     - Return the cooked sausage to the skillet. Add chicken broth, Dijon mustard, dried thyme, and ground cinnamon. Stir well to combine.
5. **Simmer:**
     - Reduce heat to low, cover, and simmer for 10-15 minutes, or until the Brussels sprouts are tender and the flavors meld together. Stir occasionally.
6. **Season and Serve:**
     - Season with salt and black pepper to taste. Garnish with chopped fresh parsley if desired.

Enjoy your savory and sweet Autumn Apple and Sausage Skillet!

Caramel Apple Cinnamon Rolls

Ingredients:

For the Dough:

- 1 cup warm milk (110°F or 45°C)
- 1/4 cup granulated sugar
- 2 1/4 teaspoons (1 packet) active dry yeast
- 1/4 cup unsalted butter, melted
- 1/4 teaspoon salt
- 1 large egg
- 3 1/2 to 4 cups all-purpose flour

For the Filling:

- 1/2 cup brown sugar, packed
- 1 tablespoon ground cinnamon
- 1/4 cup unsalted butter, softened
- 1 cup finely diced apples (peeled, cored, and preferably a tart variety like Granny Smith)

For the Caramel Sauce:

- 1/2 cup unsalted butter
- 1 cup brown sugar, packed
- 1/4 cup heavy cream
- 1/4 teaspoon vanilla extract

For the Cream Cheese Frosting (Optional):

- 4 oz (115g) cream cheese, softened
- 2 tablespoons unsalted butter, softened
- 1 cup powdered sugar
- 1/2 teaspoon vanilla extract
- 1-2 tablespoons milk (if needed to thin)

Instructions:

1. **Prepare the Dough:**
     - In a large bowl, combine warm milk and granulated sugar. Sprinkle yeast on top and let it sit for about 5 minutes, until foamy.
     - Add melted butter, salt, and egg to the yeast mixture. Mix well.
     - Gradually add flour, 1 cup at a time, until a soft dough forms. You may need more or less flour depending on the humidity.

- Turn the dough onto a floured surface and knead for about 5-7 minutes, until smooth and elastic.
- Place the dough in a greased bowl, cover with a clean towel, and let rise in a warm place for 1-2 hours, or until doubled in size.

2. **Prepare the Filling:**
   - In a small bowl, mix together brown sugar and cinnamon.
   - Punch down the risen dough and roll it out on a floured surface into a rectangle (about 12x16 inches).
   - Spread softened butter evenly over the dough.
   - Sprinkle the cinnamon-sugar mixture evenly over the butter.
   - Scatter diced apples on top.

3. **Roll and Slice:**
   - Starting from one edge, carefully roll the dough into a tight log.
   - Slice the log into 12 equal pieces and place them in a greased 9x13-inch baking dish or two greased 9-inch round pans.

4. **Second Rise:**
   - Cover the rolls with a clean towel and let them rise in a warm place for about 30 minutes, or until doubled in size.

5. **Bake:**
   - Preheat your oven to 350°F (175°C).
   - Bake the rolls for 25-30 minutes, or until golden brown and cooked through.

6. **Prepare the Caramel Sauce:**
   - While the rolls are baking, make the caramel sauce. In a saucepan, melt butter over medium heat.
   - Stir in brown sugar and bring to a simmer. Cook for about 2 minutes, then slowly stir in heavy cream. Continue cooking for another 2-3 minutes, until thickened.
   - Remove from heat and stir in vanilla extract.

7. **Prepare the Frosting (Optional):**
   - In a bowl, beat together cream cheese and butter until smooth.
   - Gradually add powdered sugar and vanilla extract, beating until combined.
   - If needed, add milk a little at a time until you reach your desired consistency.

8. **Finish and Serve:**
   - Drizzle the warm caramel sauce over the baked rolls.
   - If desired, spread the cream cheese frosting on top of the caramel sauce or serve on the side.

Enjoy your warm and gooey Caramel Apple Cinnamon Rolls!

Maple Dijon Glazed Salmon

Ingredients:

- 4 salmon fillets (6 oz each)
- 1/4 cup pure maple syrup
- 2 tablespoons Dijon mustard
- 1 tablespoon soy sauce
- 1 tablespoon olive oil
- 2 cloves garlic, minced
- 1 teaspoon dried thyme (or fresh thyme, if available)
- Salt and black pepper to taste
- Lemon wedges for serving (optional)
- Fresh parsley for garnish (optional)

Instructions:

1. **Preheat Oven:**
   - Preheat your oven to 400°F (200°C). Line a baking sheet with parchment paper or lightly grease it.
2. **Prepare the Glaze:**
   - In a small bowl, whisk together maple syrup, Dijon mustard, soy sauce, olive oil, minced garlic, and dried thyme until well combined.
3. **Season the Salmon:**
   - Season the salmon fillets with salt and black pepper on both sides.
4. **Glaze the Salmon:**
   - Place the salmon fillets on the prepared baking sheet. Brush the glaze generously over the top of each fillet.
5. **Bake:**
   - Bake in the preheated oven for 12-15 minutes, or until the salmon is cooked through and flakes easily with a fork. The glaze should be bubbly and slightly caramelized.
6. **Serve:**
   - Garnish with fresh parsley and serve with lemon wedges, if desired.

Enjoy your Maple Dijon Glazed Salmon!

Sweet Potato and Chickpea Curry

Ingredients:

- 1 tablespoon olive oil
- 1 medium onion, chopped
- 2 cloves garlic, minced
- 1 tablespoon fresh ginger, minced
- 1 tablespoon curry powder
- 1 teaspoon ground cumin
- 1/2 teaspoon ground turmeric
- 1/2 teaspoon ground cinnamon
- 1 can (14 oz) diced tomatoes
- 1 can (14 oz) coconut milk
- 2 medium sweet potatoes, peeled and diced
- 1 can (15 oz) chickpeas, drained and rinsed
- 1 cup spinach or kale, chopped
- Salt and black pepper to taste
- Fresh cilantro for garnish (optional)
- Cooked rice or naan bread for serving

Instructions:

1. **Sauté Aromatics:**
   - Heat olive oil in a large pot or Dutch oven over medium heat. Add chopped onion and cook until softened, about 5 minutes.
   - Stir in minced garlic and ginger, and cook for another 1-2 minutes.
2. **Add Spices:**
   - Add curry powder, ground cumin, ground turmeric, and ground cinnamon to the pot. Cook, stirring constantly, for 1 minute to toast the spices.
3. **Build the Base:**
   - Pour in diced tomatoes and coconut milk, stirring to combine.
   - Bring to a simmer.
4. **Add Vegetables:**
   - Add diced sweet potatoes to the pot. Stir well and cover. Simmer for about 15 minutes, or until sweet potatoes are tender.
5. **Add Chickpeas:**
   - Stir in chickpeas and cook for an additional 5 minutes to heat through.
6. **Add Greens:**
   - Stir in chopped spinach or kale and cook for another 2-3 minutes until wilted. Season with salt and black pepper to taste.
7. **Serve:**
   - Garnish with fresh cilantro, if desired.
   - Serve over cooked rice or with naan bread.

Enjoy your comforting and delicious Sweet Potato and Chickpea Curry!

Cranberry Almond Energy Bars

Ingredients:

- 1 cup almonds, chopped
- 1 cup dried cranberries
- 1 cup rolled oats
- 1/2 cup almond butter (or peanut butter)
- 1/4 cup honey or maple syrup
- 1/4 cup chia seeds (optional)
- 1/2 teaspoon vanilla extract
- A pinch of salt

Instructions:

1. **Prepare the Pan:**
    - Line an 8x8-inch baking dish with parchment paper, leaving a bit of an overhang for easy removal.
2. **Mix Dry Ingredients:**
    - In a large bowl, combine chopped almonds, dried cranberries, rolled oats, and chia seeds (if using).
3. **Prepare the Binding Mixture:**
    - In a small saucepan, gently heat almond butter and honey (or maple syrup) over low heat until melted and combined. Stir in vanilla extract and a pinch of salt.
4. **Combine:**
    - Pour the almond butter mixture over the dry ingredients. Stir well until everything is evenly coated.
5. **Press and Chill:**
    - Transfer the mixture to the prepared baking dish. Press it down firmly and evenly using a spatula or the back of a spoon.
6. **Chill and Cut:**
    - Refrigerate for at least 1 hour to set. Once firm, lift the bars out of the dish using the parchment paper and cut into squares or bars.
7. **Store:**
    - Store in an airtight container at room temperature for up to a week, or refrigerate for longer shelf life.

Enjoy your nutritious and delicious Cranberry Almond Energy Bars!

Baked Pumpkin Donuts

Ingredients:

For the Donuts:

- 1 1/2 cups all-purpose flour
- 1/2 cup granulated sugar
- 1/2 cup packed brown sugar
- 1 teaspoon baking powder
- 1/2 teaspoon baking soda
- 1/2 teaspoon ground cinnamon
- 1/4 teaspoon ground nutmeg
- 1/4 teaspoon ground ginger
- 1/2 teaspoon salt
- 1/2 cup canned pumpkin puree
- 1/4 cup milk
- 1/4 cup unsalted butter, melted
- 1 large egg
- 1 teaspoon vanilla extract

For the Cinnamon Sugar Coating (optional):

- 1/4 cup granulated sugar
- 1 tablespoon ground cinnamon
- 2 tablespoons unsalted butter, melted

Instructions:

1. **Preheat Oven:**
    - Preheat your oven to 350°F (175°C). Grease a donut pan or lightly coat it with non-stick spray.
2. **Mix Dry Ingredients:**
    - In a large bowl, whisk together flour, granulated sugar, brown sugar, baking powder, baking soda, cinnamon, nutmeg, ginger, and salt.
3. **Mix Wet Ingredients:**
    - In another bowl, combine pumpkin puree, milk, melted butter, egg, and vanilla extract. Mix well.
4. **Combine and Fill Pan:**
    - Gently fold the wet ingredients into the dry ingredients until just combined. Be careful not to overmix.
    - Spoon or pipe the batter into the prepared donut pan, filling each cavity about 2/3 full.
5. **Bake:**

    - Bake for 12-15 minutes, or until a toothpick inserted into the center comes out clean. Let cool in the pan for a few minutes, then transfer to a wire rack to cool completely.
6. **Optional Coating:**
    - If desired, mix sugar and cinnamon in a small bowl. Brush the cooled donuts with melted butter, then dip them in the cinnamon sugar mixture to coat.

Enjoy your warm, spiced Baked Pumpkin Donuts!

Harvest Fruit Crisp

Ingredients:

For the Filling:

- 4 cups mixed fruit (e.g., apples, pears, berries, peaches), peeled and chopped if needed
- 1/4 cup granulated sugar
- 1 tablespoon all-purpose flour
- 1 teaspoon ground cinnamon
- 1/4 teaspoon ground nutmeg
- 1 tablespoon lemon juice

For the Crisp Topping:

- 1/2 cup old-fashioned rolled oats
- 1/2 cup all-purpose flour
- 1/3 cup brown sugar, packed
- 1/4 cup unsalted butter, cold and cut into small pieces
- 1/4 teaspoon salt

Instructions:

1. **Preheat Oven:**
    - Preheat your oven to 350°F (175°C). Grease a 9x9-inch baking dish or similar-sized dish.
2. **Prepare the Filling:**
    - In a large bowl, combine the mixed fruit, granulated sugar, flour, cinnamon, nutmeg, and lemon juice. Toss to coat evenly.
    - Transfer the fruit mixture to the prepared baking dish.
3. **Prepare the Crisp Topping:**
    - In a separate bowl, mix together oats, flour, brown sugar, and salt.
    - Cut in the cold butter with a pastry cutter or your fingers until the mixture resembles coarse crumbs.
4. **Assemble and Bake:**
    - Sprinkle the crisp topping evenly over the fruit filling.
    - Bake in the preheated oven for 35-40 minutes, or until the topping is golden brown and the fruit filling is bubbling.
5. **Cool and Serve:**
    - Allow the crisp to cool slightly before serving. It's wonderful on its own or with a scoop of vanilla ice cream.

Enjoy your delicious Harvest Fruit Crisp!